BRAZIL

UNPACKED

Susie Brooks

Published in paperback in 2014 by Wayland
Copyright © Wayland 2014

Wayland
338 Euston Road
London NW1 3BH

Wayland Australia
Level 17/207 Kent Street
Sydney, NSW 2000

Editors: Annabel Stones and Elizabeth Brent
Designer: Peter Clayman
Cover design: Matthew Kelly

Dewey categorisation: 981'.066-dc23

ISBN 978 0 7502 8402 8

Printed in China

10 9 8 7 6 5 4 3

Picture acknowledgements: All images (including cover) and graphic elements courtesy
of Shutterstock except: p6 (right) © Peter McBride/Aurora Photos/Corbis; p7 (right) ©
peeterv/iStockphoto; p7 (left bottom) © iuoman/iStockphoto; p11 (right) © RichVintage/
iStockphoto; p12 Steven © Vidler/Eurasia Press/Corbis; p13 (top left cutout) © RollingEarth/
iStockphoto; p14 (right) © bloodstone/iStockphoto; p14 (left) © NTCo/iStockphoto; p15
(right) © merlion/iStockphoto; p16 (top) © deeAuvil/iStockphoto; p17 (bottom main) © Danny
Lehman/Corbis; pp20–21 (main) © Anthony Asael/Art in All of Us/Corbis; p21 (bottom right)
& p32 © JohannesCompaan/iStockphoto; p24 © Ricardo Azoury/CORBiS; p25 (bottom) ©
YASUYOSHi CHiBA/AFP/Getty images; p25 (top) © Globo via Getty images.

Wayland is a division of Hachette Children's Books, an Hachette UK company.
www.hachette.co.uk

Contents

Brazil: Unpacked

Welcome to Brazil, the BIG country with an even BIGGER personality! Covering nearly half of South America, it's full of party people, gigantic jungles and chock-a-block cities. It's seen some of the best footballers in history and some of the sparkliest street parades on Earth. So if you want to samba in sequins, gallop with cowboys or dodge deadly piranhas, step this way. You're in for an ENORMOUS adventure!

UNPACKED

Fact File

Flag:

Area: 8,514,877km^2
Population: 201,009,622 (July 2013 est.)
Capital city: Brasília
Land Borders: 16,885km with ten countries
Currency: the Real (R$)

Brazil

Useful Phrases

Olá - Hello (informal)
Tudo bem? - How's it going? (Answer: **Tudo bem!**)
Obrigado (boy) or Obrigada (girl) - Thank you
De nada - You're welcome
Meu nome é... - My name is...
Não entendo - I don't understand
Fala inglés? - Do you speak English?
Até depois! - See you later!

Things you will hear a lot:

Lindo maravilhoso - literally means 'beautifully marvellous' and is a good thing to say if you like something!
É mesmo - REALLY? This is the reaction you get when you've just told someone an interesting fact!

$1,2

CITY PASS

It's the most poisonous thing on eight legs... don't step on a Brazilian wandering spider!

It took British adventurer Ed Stafford 860 days, about 50,000 mozzie bites, 600 wasp stings and 12 scorpion stings to walk the length of the Amazon River!

A World of Faces

They say that in Brazil you can see all the faces of the world! Well, maybe not all of them - but it's hard to find a more varied population or such a massive melting pot of cultures. The story of Brazil's people – nearly 200 million of them – comes from many different corners of the globe. Today, Brazilians form the fifth-largest population on the planet!

First to Arrive

When Portuguese explorers arrived in Brazil in 1500, they got a big surprise. A group of men, armed with bows and arrows, were already there! In fact there were probably 1,000 tribes living in Brazil by then. They spoke a range of languages that the Portuguese couldn't understand.

The arrival of Europeans spelled trouble for indigenous tribes.

Changing Faces

Things changed when the Portuguese settled. They forced indigenous people to work on sugar plantations, and shipped in slaves from Africa too. Thousands of natives died due to cruelty or European diseases. From the late 1800s, the mix of people grew wider as workers from Europe, Japan and Russia flocked to join in the coffee and rubber trades. If you enjoy a pizza or sushi in Brazil, it's this wave of immigrants you can thank!

NO WAY!

There are more people of Lebanese origin in Brazil than in Lebanon itself!

You earn your fish supper if you catch it this way.

The Mix Today

Over the years, many immigrants, indigenous people and Africans intermarried – and that's why the population is so diverse today. Most Brazilians are descended from Europeans or mixed European and indigenous families, but there are many other groups too. Deep in the Amazon, tribes still hunt with arrows and build shelters out of palms. Some remain completely out of touch with the rest of the world.

It's a multiethnic society, but everyone's proud to be Brazilian!

Let's go to Rio!

Once Brazil's capital and now the most visited city in the southern hemisphere, Rio de Janeiro is a true crowd pleaser! Its beautiful beaches, breathtaking views and colourful Carnival attract more than 1.5 million tourists a year. Rio is home to 7 million fun-lovers, a sunny outdoor lifestyle and Brazil's biggest sports stadium. No wonder it was picked to host the 2016 Olympic Games!

Christ the Redeemer

Arms outstretched (and, as cheeky locals say, ready to clap for his favourite samba school) *Cristo Redentor* is the face of Rio. Standing 30m tall and weighing 700 tons, this iconic statue was hauled up Corcovado Mountain by rail. Visitors can ride a cogwheel train, then climb 220 steps – or take the escalator! – to his feet. It's worth it for spectacular views of the city.

With arms spanning 28m, he could give you one gigantic hug!

Rio de Janeiro means 'January River' in Portuguese.

Despite its name Rio is built on a bay, not a river!

Heights and Sights

To see Rio from another height, take a cable car up Sugar Loaf Mountain. Adventurous types can climb up or rappel down this 396m peak. Stretching out below, famous beaches like Ipanema and Copacabana offer kilometres of bright sand and surf. And in Tijuca, the world's largest urban forest, you can paraglide or zipline through the leafy jungle canopy. Look out for monkeys as you go!

Going for Gold

In 2016, South America's first ever Olympic and Paralympic Games will come to Rio. More than 10,500 athletes from 205 countries are expected to join in, and the race is on to prepare the city for crowds of international fans. Sixteen new venues and an Olympic Village housing 17,700 beds are being built. With a nation of sports stars and supporters behind it, Rio really will be going for gold!

Rio beat Tokyo, Chicago and Madrid to win the Olympic bid.

Viva Futebol!

If there's one thing that stops the nation in Brazil, it's football! People are so crazy for it that businesses and banks often shut during major games. Nowhere else has a better track record in the FIFA World Cup, which comes to Rio in 2014. Other sports, such as volleyball, motor racing and sailing, are popular here too - but nothing matches the religion they call *futebol*!

Prepare for loud cheers, loud music and tooting car horns when Brazil wins a game!

World Cup Winners

In 2002, Brazil claimed its fifth World Cup title – a record in the history of the tournament. The famous yellow shirts have been runners up twice, but coming second is like losing to Brazilians! In 2014 they'll be looking to reclaim the top spot in Rio's revamped Maracanã Stadium. This was built for the 1950 World Cup and is one of the biggest sports venues in the world.

Street Start

How do stars like Ronaldinho, Kaká and Neymar develop their fast-paced style? By starting young! Football comes as naturally as walking to children all around Brazil. You'll see them playing barefoot on streets, beaches, wastelands...any patch of ground they can find. If there's no ball, no problem – a drinks can, rock or lunchbox will do!

Pelé Pride

When asked how you spell Pelé, one journalist summed it up: 'G-O-D'! Although he hung up his boots in the 1970s, this flawless forward will forever be a national hero. Pelé helped Brazil to three World Cup victories and scored a whopping 1,281 goals in his career.

They say playing barefoot is good for your dribbling skills!

Kaká was the first ever athlete to score 10 million followers on Twitter.

NO WAY!

On World Cup Final day in 1950, the Maracanã Stadium seated a crowd of 200,000 fans - the most ever recorded at a football match. Unfortunately, Brazil didn't win!

Jungle Giant

Brazil is so huge that the whole of non-Russian Europe would fit within it! It's 35 TIMES the size of the UK. The country crosses three time zones, which means at 11am in Manaus, it's midday in Brasília and 1pm on the islands of Fernando de Noronha. Brazil has nearly a quarter of Earth's fresh water running through it, and enough forest to cover most of India. Don't get lost!

NO WAY!

The Amazon River starts in Peru and carries more water than any other river in the world. Straightened out, it would stretch from New York, USA, to Berlin, Germany!

It's a wiggly 6,400km trip down the Amazon River.

Taller than Niagara and far wider, the Iguaçu Falls join Brazil and Argentina.

Highs and Lows

South of Amazonia, the Planalto is a vast upland area where you'll find dramatic red-rock canyons and waterfalls. It's breezier up here, with cool, wet winters and hot summers. In the sunny north-east, droughts can strike but there are beautiful sandy beaches and dunes. Fernando de Noronha, a short flight off the coast, is an island paradise where turtles, sharks – and surfers – all thrive.

Southern Swamps

Every rainy season, a web of rivers in south-west Brazil burst their banks, flood the land and leave behind small islands. This is the Pantanal, the world's largest wetland area and once an inland sea. There are few people and no towns here – but keep an eye out for cowboys (*peões*). It's one of the best places in Brazil for spotting animals and birds. You can even fish for piranhas if you dare!

In the Pantanal waters you'll find fishy friends...and foes!

A-MAZE-ing Amazonia

If you set out alone in Amazonia, you almost certainly WOULD get lost. The rivers and rainforests of this maze-like region cover nearly half of Brazil. In the tropical jungle it's hot, humid and wet all year. Trekkers need machetes to hack paths through the dense vegetation. It's a wildlife haven too, though anacondas, caimans and electric eels aren't the friendliest neighbours to have around...

The piranha has razor-sharp teeth and a mighty appetite.

Nature's Treasure

ew places on Earth are as rich in nature as Brazil. About a tenth of all animal species and at least 50,000 types of plant are found in the rainforests alone. Everything grows here, from cotton to exotic fruits, and wildlife can be wonderful, deadly or weird...

A Victoria Amazonica water lily is very hard to miss – its leaves can span for 3m and hold the weight of a small animal or child.

A bullet ant's sting is said to be as painful as a gunshot.

This sticky white juice is latex, being tapped from a rubber tree. Indigenous people used to dip their feet in it to make shoes! Nowadays it's vulcanised to make all sorts of rubber stuff.

The world's largest rodent, the capybara, is like a giant, water-going guinea pig. It has webbed feed for swimming and diving and can hold its breath for up to five minutes.

Pink dolphins can be found in the Amazon River. They have brains 40 per cent bigger than ours!

Brazil nuts grow in pods on wild Amazon trees, and every nut you eat is hand-collected. Workers know when they're ripe because the pods drop down – bad news if you're standing underneath!

Highways and Skyways

Overnight buses are big in Brazil - not surprising, given the huge distances! Surfaces can be bumpy and traffic heavy, but with a limited rail network most people take to the roads. A quicker option is to fly between cities, though the main air hubs are in the south so you may have to make a detour. Traveller's tip: pack patience and enjoy the adventure!

River Roads

When you're deep in the jungle or rains flood the roads, the only way to travel is by boat. Passengers cruise the Amazon River on ferries slung with hammocks, blaring out music, movies and live shows. Barges carry cargo, such as timber or minerals, and fishing boats chug their catch to market ports. A school run might be done in a dugout canoe – just hollow out a tree trunk and paddle!

Riverboats wait for passengers at the port city of Manaus.

Sugar Cane Cars

Who would have thought you could use sugar to run a car? Well you almost can! In Brazil the majority of cars are 'flexi-fuel', running on ethanol – produced from sugar cane – and traditional fuel. Biodiesel, made from soybeans, is also churned out in this country. Another local product benefits the motor industry too – rubber! Most major tyre companies have factories in Brazil, and more than 3 million vehicles are manufactured here each year.

Packed with energy, sugar cane produces sugar for you, or ethanol for your car!

Big trips!

→ **Rio**
↓ (about 2,400km)
• by bus: 50 hours
• by air: 3.5 hours

Belém
↓ (about 1,300km)
• by riverboat: 4–6 days
• by air: 2 hours

Manaus

Heli-Capital

Guzzling green fuel is one thing, but many Brazilian cities are still polluted places, choked with gridlocked traffic. In São Paulo, where hundreds of new cars join the roads each day, jams can build up to 295km – that's further than London to Manchester, UK! Wealthy businesspeople dodge the mayhem by flitting about in helicopters instead. This city has more private choppers than any other in the world, and a mass of helipads on its rooftops.

Sit in the world's worst traffic jams – or fly above them!

17

Bright Lights, Big Cities

Noisy, hectic and huge, Brazil's cities can be daunting places. More than 170 million Brazilians now live in them - a big contrast to 50 years ago, when two-thirds of the population were rural. Brasília, the capital, is the largest city in the world that didn't exist before 1900 - 2.6 million people now call it home. In São Paulo, more than 11 million *Paulistanos* go about their daily lives.

São Paulo is known for its high-rise buildings and non-stop lifestyle!

Spectacular Sampa

São Paulo (or *Sampa*, as locals call it) is Brazil's biggest, busiest and richest city. With 280 cinemas, 120 concert halls, 71 museums, 15,000 bars and 12,500 restaurants, residents aren't short of things to do. *Paulistanos* are hard workers – even workaholics – according to the laid-back *Cariocas* of Rio! A wealth of immigrant cultures means there's never a dull moment on more than 91,000 city streets.

Brasília's cathedral is designed to look like hands praying.

Favela Living

Not everyone can afford a chic city lifestyle. About 12 million Brazilians live in slums called *favelas*, where housing is makeshift and poor. Crime is a problem here, and health standards low, but spirits are often still high. Many residents are trying to improve things with creative schemes and businesses, such as surf schools, music groups and craft shops. Visitors can pay to look round some *favelas* on a supervised, whistlestop tour.

The architects who designed Brasília picked a futuristic design for the modern capital – from the air, it looks like an aeroplane! The city was built from scratch in just four years. Impressive, given that when work started the nearest railway was 175km away and the nearest paved road more than 400km beyond that. Brasília is home to the national government, plus a natty range of buildings that have made it a World Heritage Site.

Favela houses teeter on steep hillsides around Rio.

NO WAY!

São Paulo has the largest community of Japanese people outside Japan AND Italians outside Italy.

Being Brazilian

Life can be fast, fun or painfully frustrating in Brazil. While beachside bars buzz with rich revellers, poor farmers struggle to eat. Contrasts between city and rural living are huge, but some things are true countrywide. Brazilians are friendly, family-loving people who will give you a great welcome - just don't be surprised if they're late!

School Shifts

Imagine starting your school day at 7am. That's normal for children in Brazil – some even have their breakfast in the classroom! Shortages of equipment and teachers mean that lessons often work in shifts, with morning pupils stopping at noon and a new group arriving after lunch. Education is free until the age of 14, but many kids skip school and go to work to earn money for their families.

About 98% of Brazil's young people are now able to read and write.

All in Good Faith

If you see people making offerings to the sea in Brazil, they're probably practising Candomblé. This Afro-Brazilian faith is just one of a vast range of religions here. About 123 million Brazilians are Roman Catholics – no other country has as many. Brazil is also home to Evangelical Protestants, Buddhists, Muslims... and record numbers of Kardecian Spiritists, who believe in communicating with the dead.

The Goddess of the Sea is loaded with gifts at the Candomblé Yemanjá festival.

NO WAY!

Brazil is a land of young people, with 24% of the population under the age of 14 and 62% under 29!

Cowboy Culture

Herding cattle can be a tough job – but in a country that exports more beef than any other, it's part of the way of life. Cowboys strut their stuff across rural Brazil, their style varying from region to region. Northern *vaqueiros* wear leather clothing for protection as they charge through thorny scrub. Baggy-trousered *gauchos* ride the southern grasslands, and test their guts (and grip!) at white-knuckle rodeos.

A straw hat is the style for cowboys in the Pantanal.

Looking Good

Some say that many Brazilians can't walk past a mirror without looking in it. *Vaidade*, or vanity, is no bad thing as far as they're concerned! Looking good and keeping fit are so much a part of Brazil's culture that even beaches are dotted with gyms. The beauty industry is booming, fashions are jaw-droppingly daring, and Brazilian designers and supermodels are taking the world by storm.

Rio's white sands are littered with perfect beach bodies!

Beach Babes

Brazilian women go to the beach to be seen – and in the typical teeny 'dental floss' bikini, wobbly bits are not an option! People exercise fanatically to keep themselves in perfect shape, and many take things even further. Plastic surgery has become a multibillion-dollar industry here, with more than 5,000 registered surgeons nipping and tucking cosmetic tourists from around the world.

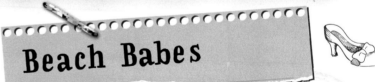

International Style

For Brazilian beauties like Gisele Bündchen, looking good comes naturally. She tops the bill as the highest-paid supermodel in the world! Designers, such as Gloria Coelho and her son Pedro Lourenço, have shot to global stardom, and fashion weeks in Rio and São Paulo are now the fifth-largest on the international scene. Raking in more than £40 million a year and employing nearly 2 million people, Brazil's fashion industry is...well...not just a pretty face.

Gisele struts her stuff in Brazilian fashion label Colcci.

NO WAY!

Many people worry about having a big bottom, but the Brazilian Butt Lift involves injecting more fat into your behind! Surprisingly, it's one of the most popular cosmetic operations.

Traditional Dress

Big, frilly dresses aren't for everyone – but Baiana women wear them with pride! Their style has African roots and features a long, full skirt made of lace or embroidered fabric and worn with a shawl, turban and beads. Brazilians care about tradition, and in the multiethnic south you'll see costumes from Germany, Italy, Japan and more. Of course, in the Amazon, there are tribes who prefer to wear no clothes at all...

Baiana people come from Bahia, a region in northern Brazil.

Arts for All

In a country full of colour and beauty, the art scene has a head-start. Wacky painters, historic sculptors, creative writers, architects and filmmakers from Brazil have all captured the world's imagination over the years. From traditional weavings to modern graffiti, Brazilians have an eye for the arts. Even those who don't like museums can find their own form of culture on TV!

On the Wall

The first artists to paint on walls in Brazil lived more than 25,000 years ago. In the caves of Serra de Capivara, you can still see their pictures today. Elsewhere in Brazil, walls scream with modern *grafite* – now a serious art form that has even been legalised in Rio. Street artists like Cranio take their spray cans all around the world. His trademark blue characters show indigenous people, painted into jungles of a different, concrete kind.

It's ancient graffiti – Brazil's rock art includes doodles of deer and lizards.

TV Talent

Though not strictly art, Brazilians might call their *telenovelas* masterpieces! These dramatic soap operas attract more than 40 million viewers a day – and that's just in their home country. Around 2,500 hours of soaps are filmed each year, from an impressive studio site in Rio's Atlantic forest. Brazilians love the storylines and characters because they reflect real life. Many *telenovelas* have international fan bases too.

Football legend Pelé cameos in a Brazilian soap!

NO WAY!

The soap *Avenida Brasil* was so popular that even the President changed her plans. She cancelled a rally that clashed with the final episode - lucky, because a record 80 million viewers tuned in!

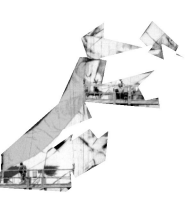

A fine place for a portrait of Brazilian architect, Oscar Niemeyer!

Off the Wall

Decorating London, UK, with 10,000 coloured paper bananas is one way of showing your art abroad! Breno Pineschi did this in 2012, spreading the cheer of his hometown Rio. Fellow Brazilian Vik Muniz prefers to make his art with spaghetti...dirt...sugar...even diamonds! He once copied the Mona Lisa using peanut butter and jam, and made a portrait of Elvis Presley out of chocolate.

Adventurous Tastes

If you're invited for lunch in a Brazilian home, don't expect a quick snack. Mealtimes in Brazil are more-the-merrier affairs, where families often sit, chat and laugh for hours. Food is as varied as the cultures across the country, but you won't get far without trying rice and beans. Mix them with pigs' feet, ears, tail and snout (if you're brave enough) and you've got Brazil's national dish!

Fancy Feijoada

Feijoada, the national dish, is a rich stew of black beans and meat. Now often made with smoked pork (no scary bits!), it's served with bowls of rice, toasted manioc flour, fried kale and slices of orange. Most people save their feijoada fix for weekends, when there's time to cook and enjoy it. It's definitely a lunchtime meal – far too filling to eat before going to bed!

Fresh pork, dried beef, smoked sausage... feijoada is like a meaty lucky dip!

Home-grown Flavours

When it comes to local produce, it's hard to beat Brazil. About a third of the world's coffee is grown here, and people will drink it at any time of day. Pequi, pitanga, cagaita...never heard of them? They're just some of many thousands of exotic native fruits. Enjoy them fresh, juiced or turned into ice cream – açaí, one of the most popular, will give you an energy boost!

Anyone for palm fruits, coconuts, guavas, cacao, cupuaçu...?

Açaí berries

Snack Attack

You're never far from a snack on Brazil's streets and beaches. Here are just a few speedy treats:

Pastel – a deep-fried dumpling, filled with anything from cheese, fish or meat to chocolate.

Tacacá – a broth made with manioc, shrimps and jambu – a leaf that makes your mouth tingle.

Pamonha – boiled, stuffed corn husks, traditionally sold from vans playing a musical chant.

Wash it down with...
sugarcane juice, coconut water, or a can of fizzy Guaraná. Coffee has to be *cafezinho* – short, sweet and strong!

Pequi fruit

Pamonha

Pastel

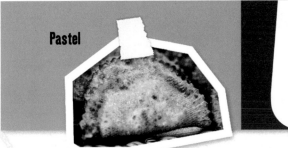

Prepare to Party!

Feet stomping, hips swaying, arms twirling and music thumping, Brazilians can party like none other! The sounds, moves and rhythms of the country are a mash-up of traditions from around the world. Every dance tells a story, every tune has heart and soul… and every festival gets the nation on their feet. If a quiet time is what you're after, Brazil's clubs and Carnival are not for you!

Kicking Capoeira

When African slaves were forbidden to fight, they invented Capoeira instead! This musical form of martial arts tricked slave owners into thinking they were dancing. A high-kicking, acrobatic and gymnastic extravaganza, Capoeira is usually performed in a circle. Dancers take it in turns to go in the middle and 'fight', while others play music and sing songs. A bow-based instrument called the berimbau sets the pace.

More than 70 samba schools compete in the Rio Carnival. With 3,000 – 5,000 dancers apiece, that's a LOT of feathers and feet!

In Capoeira you have to kick high and duck fast!

Sultry Samba

You might know someone who's been to samba lessons – Brazil's energetic dance style is now shaking bottoms around the world! It's danced to an African-style rhythm, beaten out by a double-headed drum and all sorts of percussion and string instruments. Dancers wear bright, skimpy costumes and have to perfect the 'samba bounce', which is more of a knee-flex than a jump.

Carnival Crazy

Every year, 40 days before Easter, Brazil bursts into even more life than usual. Carnival fever erupts across the country and lasts for almost a week. Samba schools in Rio, each with their own distinctive style, spend the year practising, writing music and designing glitzy costumes and floats. Then they take to the streets to compete in spectacular parades. You can dress up and march with them if you like!

Rio's world-famous Carnival is a whirl of music and dance!

TALENTO VERDADEIRO

More Information

Websites

http://www.kidscornerbrazil.org
Facts, games and a virtual tour of Brazil!

http://www.rio2016.org.br/en
The official site of the Rio Olympic and Paralympic Games.

http://www.lonelyplanet.com/brazil
All you need to prepare for a trip to Brazil.

http://www.celebratebrazil.com/
A personal account of the Brazilian people and culture.

http://www.riocarnival.net
Carnival parades, street parties, samba schools...read all about them here!

Apps

Brazil Shaker by Phonecast Solutions
Shake your iPhone or iPod to play the maracas and other instruments in time with Brazilian music!

Brazil Quest by Monumenta Comunicação e Estratégias Sociais
Visit 12 Brazilian cities and help lost alien Yep complete his challenges!

Brazil Travel Guide by Travel Guides
Brazil at your fingertips, an Android app.

Learn Portuguese - MindSnacks by MindSnacks
A fun and free way to learn Portuguese!

Movies

Rio, 20th Century Fox, 2011 (U)
A nerdy bird who can't fly embarks on a wild adventure in the Amazon jungle. A fun animated film, by the makers of Ice Age.

Brazil with Michael Palin, BBC, 2012 (12)
Explore Brazil and meet its people in this fascinating travel documentary.

Rio 2, 20th Century Fox, 2014 (U)
The sequel to the much loved 2011 film.

Clips

http://kids.nationalgeographic.co.uk/kids/places/find/brazil/
Click on the Video tab to tour Brazil's cities, forests, wetlands, Carnival and much more.

http://www.bbc.co.uk/worldclass/16657170
Visit a favela in Rio and join its children at surf school!

http://www.bbc.co.uk/learningzone/clips/brazilian-soccer-skills-combinations/6319.html
Pick up some Brazilian football tips!

http://www.bbc.co.uk/learningzone/clips/samba-an-introduction/8795.html
Learn some smooth samba moves from a Brazilian carnival group.

Books

Countries Around the World: Brazil by Marion Morrison
(Raintree, 2011)

Countries in Our World: Brazil by Edward Parker
(Franklin Watts, 2012)

Developing World: Brazil and Rio De Janeiro
by Louise Spilsbury (Franklin Watts, 2013)

Radar: Dance Culture: Capoeira by Liz Gogerly
(Wayland, 2011)

Swing 'n' Sleep
Tip: If you string up a hammock in the Brazilian jungle, lie in it diagonally for the best night's sleep!

Glossary

Amazonia The area surrounding the Amazon River, made up mainly of rainforest. It covers most of northern Brazil and extends into several neighbouring countries.

anaconda A large snake from the boa family that coils around and crushes its prey.

caiman A meat-eating, alligator-like reptile.

cosmetic tourist Someone who travels for cosmetic surgery.

favelas Brazilian shanty towns, usually found on the outskirts of major cities.

immigrants People who come to a new country to live.

indigenous Native to a particular place.

machete A large, heavy knife with a wide blade.

manioc A type of root that can be cooked and eaten or ground to make flour.

rappel To slide down a rock face using a rope.

rodeo An event where cowboys display their skills at riding bucking horses and roping cattle.

rural Relating to the countryside, rather than towns.

southern hemisphere The southern half of the globe, below the equator.

vulcanise To strengthen natural rubber by adding chemicals.

Index